Mutton Rolls

Arji Manuelpillai

Published by Out-Spoken Press,
Unit 39, Containerville
1 Emma Street
London, E2 9FP

First edition published 2020
ISBN: 978-1-9160468-7-0

Artwork: Zoe Norvell

Printed & Bound by: Print Resource

Typeset in: Adobe Caslon

Out-Spoken Press is supported using public funding by the National Lottery through Arts Council England.

Supported using public funding by
ARTS COUNCIL
ENGLAND

Mutton Rolls

Arji Manuelpillai

OUT SPOKEN PRESS

Out-Spoken Press
London

Acknowledgements

These poems belong to all the people who inspired and assisted me along my journey. Firstly, my family for all their support. Anna for putting up with me, Sophia Nicholson for her thoughtful eye, BPMoore for the support. To all the tutors who gave up their time and energy to push me forward, especially Hannah Lowe, Wayne Holloway-Smith and Jonathan Edwards. Also thanks to groups including Malika's Poetry Kitchen, Stanza with Alice Hiller and The Poetry School; the moment I realised poetry was a team game was the moment the poems began to fly. Finally special thanks to the Jerwood/Arvon mentorship and to Out-Spoken Press for believing in me.

Table of Contents

credit card

someone pretended to be me
filled my details out online
intercepted the card as it arrived
and went to Morrisons. Someone

in a red sweater, NY cap
black jeans, pink socks
spent 200 quid on
groceries I imagine, booze

toothpaste, noodles, coco-pops
definitely leeks and potatoes
for a leek and potato soup
(crème fraîche to stir in)

that someone then caught
the bus, the 343 perhaps, went
to that Peckham café
on the white side of Peckham

sat on a shared table
had a tea and carrot cake
read the paper, leant
back in their seat

so their hands fell to their sides
and the lady to the right
casual as breathing
pulled her handbag close

brown boys in Kavos

It's 4am in a balmy Greek heat
four brown corduroy-coloured boys
are failing to get laid
in the 'getting laid' capital of Greece

they suck tulip-topped spliffs
sip the backwash of cheap vodka
talk cool (as brown boys do)
of not being bothered

their white friends, 'fucking 'ave it' mottos
are banging bedheads, curling tongues
sprinkling raindrops on necklines
but brown boys are not bothered

they have spent many nights
clumped in clubs, next to girls
who call them reliable and sweet
who they lead like helpful theatre ushers

across rumbling dance floors
graciously into the open arms
of black boys with large penises
sweaty charisma and beautiful blackness

then to shirtless white boys
hands-high, glitter-soaked torsos
all fearless and normal and slavemastery
brown boys think themselves ugly

but not yet ugly because they are brown
the sun is reaching over rooftops
brown boys light cigs and laugh
an orgasm is caught in the breeze

half catholic

I clasp my palms like I'm caging a fly
ironed shirt, polished school shoes

is God impressed by how I dress on Sundays?
I wonder whether that girl is

our father who art
in heaven

at fifteen I touch a man in a way
that makes me wish God didn't exist

throw up behind a Ford Fiesta
brush my teeth till the toothbrush snaps

forgive us our trespasses

in Lourdes years later
I light a candle

fingers trail rows of rusty crutches
miracles, mum says

that day, at the statue
I cry so tightly

promise not to want
a man again

please God I know I don't often come here
but if you do this one thing

candles burn out
wax crumbles off my body

like paint off the feet of Jesus
Amen

after the tsunami
I watch a man

pickpocket a corpse
quietly as though hiding it from the sky

nominated for a BAME prize

it's always in capitals
like someone is shouting it
like the bus beeping
to let the disabled ramp down

I'm at an award ceremony
there's BAME waitresses
toilet attendants, caterers
and us, like the lead parts

in *Coming to America*
sari, shalwar, hijab, turban
so many BAME outfits
I feel almost unBAME

in my M&S shirt and trousers
I am stuffed, for photos
with canapés, meat on stick
marvelling at the ceiling

tomorrow when I meet my family
I shall tell them I was loved
revered by many
I will say I drank responsibly

Cecilia says we're all fucked up

it's only when I started therapy   I realised how many people
are in therapy   like when you take magic mushrooms and start
seeing mushrooms all over the place   I don't remember my
dreams   sometimes make them up to please her   as a kid I'd
go for an eye test   learn the board just before I sat down   she
must get so tired   death and sex and death and make some
time in the day to allow yourself to be sad   that's therapist stock
material   I can see her reading me   like a public toilet door
there is a dragon I tell her   squeezing up my trachea   choking
me   it isn't easy choosing paintings for a room like this or vases
or paperweights   my friend died when I was 24 I never got
to say goodbye   I was busy being strong   that's why abstract
paintings work so well   she's leaning back   must be time   wipe
the tears away like face paint   how long before I'm wandering
drunk down the Old Kent Road   not knowing how I got there

Hawaiʻi

It isn't right to refuse a lei flower in Hawaiʻi
nor a spliff at the end of a night out

even if you know it will spin you sideways
leg dropping from the duvet like an anchor

it's old times, whiteying with you in the kitchen
forehead like the hottest and coldest day in Hawaiʻi

stifling Hawaiʻi, suffocating, room's on a selfie stick
we always do this when I think I'm going to die —

imagine Hawaiʻi, girlfriends slightly hotter than ours
a beach, not shingle but sand, a backdrop of phallic boulders

umbrellaed cocktails busier than an East London garden
honestly, it's been a struggle since she left

Hawaiʻi, a place of palm trees and coconuts
monkeys on beaches, feels like I'm falling apart

a place where they don't measure the shots in cocktails
I can't wait till we go to Hawaiʻi, mate —

I'm so lonely, garlands round our necks
my arm hung from your shoulder

raves aren't places to cry

last week, in a club's toilet cubicle
I ate a photo of you

no one could hear me sob
beneath the hum of bass

roll one, double drop, let's get on
it holding you

all endless and infinite, holding you
security kicked the door in

carried me to the backroom
said *raves aren't places to cry*

after the Sri Lankan bombing that kills 360 (after the 20 year war that killed significantly more)

after the news   my skin feels darker   prayers for   thoughts
for   texted condolence   but the majority of my relatives are
long dead   mostly from natural causes   I'm only Sri Lankan
at weddings and funerals   or for inquisitive white people
Uncle Prithi is marked as safe   no damp tissues in this house
buffering   only slow moving heads   like watching slo-mo ping
pong   like when my brother had a splinter   I knew wouldn't
come out on its own   *downloading*   everyone on the news
looks like my uncle or aunty   cousin or nephew   but poorer
or dead   "aahh back to the ol' days" Ammama would say
buffering bathed in sun and blood   *Raj Kumar marked safe*
my uncle tells me   *typing...*   they don't need therapy in
Sri Lanka   they just get on with it   *typing...*   like taking out
the trash   *last seen 05.47*   or burying a body or detonating
a bomb in the buffet line of the Cinnamon Grand Hotel
from here (on the toilet)   it's all just a cluster of tiny red faces
wailing in a language I don't understand   in a country I can't
oh look! that's where Mama and Appa first met

white people

every sort of white people
pink as grapefruit, pinking
string-clothed, sizzling
bacon sausage
strips glistening on the grill
white people
dead on their deckchairs
cocktails and nachos
etch-a-sketch tattoos
texting *wish you were 'ere*
wonderfully wistful
white people
bee-eyed, pre-tanned
sun-creaming their screaming
4-year-old, thumbing
a Catherine Cookson classic
T-shirt saying
I went to Tenerife and all I got was
white people
bouncing bulges
kebabby chip fat
frothing from pantie lines
twitching buttocks
rabbits with nightmares
oh wonderfully
white people
return to work
smiling coyly
flashing your skin
like a fine new coat

Crufts

he's coughing   hucking up white bile   spouting out the
mouth   we're trying to watch Crufts   he's spluttering into
sick bags   dog-spotting   complimenting a chihuahua pruned
as a hedge   Aunty forcing his head through a bib   a terrier
glides in   they're arguing about what he should and shouldn't
eat   about puking on a new jumper   *take the nutritional shake
it gave Aunty Kumi five more months*   they pull the leash so
tight it's choking the poor thing   we are taking turns crying
in the bathroom   Mike is a 3-year-old Irish Water Spaniel
strutting with true grace   I disappear to wash vomit from his
slippers   I shouldn't be doing this at the kitchen sink   crying
I mean   neither should my cousin who has come to help   nor
my mother who appears behind us   motionless   a family
photo   developing in the window

regret

is my mum chatting in Tamil to the boy at the petrol station
counter

his eyes full beam, her shoulders slacken
faces into old grooves, as friends at a reunion

வாங்க ஆன்ட்டி எப்படி இருக்கிறீங்க?

she is Aunty, he is Thamby
and the queue behind us can wait

as can I, hanging between them
a wind vane trying to find the wind

      plucking subtitles from their eyebrows
            intention in the corners of their lips
    snatching at the remnants of english
        dropped like loose change

ரெண்டு மூன்று மாசமா கொஞ்சம் பிசினஸ்
குறைவு தான்

I think I got that bit…that's probably what he said

ceremonies, funerals, temple poojas
when the priest circles the burning flame
muttering the words of God
I only pray
        he does not speak to me

You no understand Tamil?

I'm caught off guard, a ghost touched
perusing the wrapper of a Lion bar

No I ...I ...

      want to flutter my english vowel sounds
    reel off Shakespeare, Biggie, Eliot
        in the voice of a newsreader

but I'm distracted by my image in the security monitor
my body shifting foot to foot
a child outside the Headmaster's office

he doesn't pause long, returning to Tamil
probably telling my mum I've forgotten my roots
and my mum nodding, probably saying
sorry, I agree, I'm embarrassed to say he's my son

we are farewelling
my mother and the boy smiling
me waving my free Lion bar at the electric door

cancer cancer cancer

when I am touching myself like this
I am either masturbating
or checking that I am not dying
suddenly

I knead the meat of my chest
follow the ticker tape along my back
fondle the pockets of my scrotum
like I am searching for change

these are monthly measures of tenderness
made daily

when it arrived that summer
aunties and uncles would console
but none would dare speak its name
now we cannot speak his

an IKEA flat pack

I am following you   up the aisle   along the checkout

sat beside you as you drive   it's in the back   bubble

wrapped   I'm tearing the box   popping bags of nuts

and bolts   but really I am admiring the neighbour's

washing line   you finger the instructions   sort

the wood by size   I'm knee bound   looking

for a screw   below the fridge   you're building

I'm carrying things   putting them down

you're building   till we argue   storm off   later

we watch a film   as the sex scene creeps in   we fall

to thick silence   your eyes   look anywhere but me

like I'm your dog   shitting   we cannot find

the shape our fingers used to fit   so I compliment

our IKEA shelving unit   that night   I dream we are

standing in the pouring rain pretending not to get wet

after being called a paki

my father used to say
the hardest oranges to peel
are often the sweetest

when he first came to England
he worked double the hours
took the jobs no one else would

when his roommate was beaten
outside Vauxhall tube station
he hardly spoke for a month

my father told him *knuckle down*
the only answer was
to work harder

tonight when I tell
my father what happened
he covers his mouth

with his hand
an orange peel attaching
back onto an orange

obviously my girlfriend is the best

my sister-in-law meanders in
later than our family usually get up
her body pokes through pyjamas
like furniture under sheets
she kisses him
luxuriously long
Mama searches for a pot
that doesn't exist

when everyone is ready to leave
she announces she will not be coming
it's just too hot for us
we are a shoal of startled fish
they are playing in the pool
like two crossed lovers
travelling through
a plughole

after they have gone to bed
the family dissect their canoodling
how she lays in his arms
like Cleopatra in milk
how she fails to call Mama *Aunty*
and doesn't eat hot food
Mama speaks quietly
like a hurricane that hasn't yet hit

monkey

look at me
flying through the window so the whole pub screams
smashing the bottles off the back of the bar
scattering pork scratchings on your good ol' days

look at me
death-staring that small child
while I yank off the dart board
frisbee it at the wise-crack just out the toilet

climbing the walls then sliding my red balls
up and down the length of the TV
so everyone can see these scarlet arse cheeks
the pixelated Harry Kane making that fingers-on-plate sound

look at me, bowling pool balls
at old folks with older jokes about onion bhajis
spearing the pool stick into your bulldog's butt
NO! I will not keep calm and carry on I'll rip

the flag from the wall
swing circles on the chandelier
mane in wind, voice echoing with that joyful mantra
of brown boys in the countryside

S. S. Industries (after the '83 riots)

my grandfather built a factory
a castle framed by Colombo smog
brick-walled, thick as biceps taut
figures in windows, irises in his eyes

my grandfather built a factory
the rooms like pulsing organs
ironclad chimneys scribbling
his signature on the dotted skyline

my grandfather built a factory
stainless steel pots, pans, plates
gleaming medals in our kitchen
my mum holding them high shouting

your grandfather built a factory!
she says it sang with his being, growled
with his grit, whistled like his workers
so the city always remembers

my grandfather built a factory
that was burnt to black by thugs
and for my whole life, my grandfather
never spoke another word

because it's in the Lonely Planet top five places to visit

she is telling me how he asked her   at sunset   as the sun
licked the sea red   and the birds punched shrapnel in the sky
she suspected something as he disappeared   just as their song
sang from the beach hut   how he knelt into a sandy dune
where Tigers once rested their rifles   and metallic shells were
plucked like poppies in the wake   how tears swallowed his
words   will you —   I used to march to make change   but
since then   I march just to sleep at night   that country
changed me she says   the bars the sea-views biryani kothu roti
plus the people are so generous   they don't hassle like Indians
they'd drop a bomb   wait five minutes   drop another to
kill the rescue party   they spent that whole evening staring
out to sea   she says it's their paradise   they made a pact to
go back every ten years   to that bar   in that country where
bombs rained in no fire zones   where bodies are hidden sixty
to a hole   it's hard to put into words   he says as their fingers
weave together   it's somewhere we could call our second
home   the soldiers were spread across Tamil land   few tried
for war crimes   I don't know why you don't move back there

Other titles by Out-Spoken Press

Contains Mild Peril • FRAN LOCK

Epiphaneia • RICHARD GEORGES

Stage Invasion: Poetry & the Spoken Word Renaissance
PETE BEARDER

Nascent • VOL I: A BAME ANTHOLOGY

Ways of Coping • OLLIE O'NEILL

The Neighbourhood • HANNAH LOWE

The Games • HARRY JOSEPHINE GILES

Songs My Enemy Taught Me • JOELLE TAYLOR

To Sweeten Bitter • RAYMOND ANTROBUS

Dogtooth • FRAN LOCK

How You Might Know Me • SABRINA MAHFOUZ

Heterogeneous, New & Selected Poems
ANTHONY ANAXAGOROU

Titanic • BRIDGET MINAMORE

Email: press@outspokenldn.com